The Great Gift Exchange

An Easy-to-sing, Easy-to-stage Kids' Christmas Musical about the Saving Gift of Jesus

Created by Carter Robertson

Performance time: 27 minutes

Copyright © 2009 by PsalmSinger Music, Box 419527, Kansas City, MO 64141.
All rights reserved. Litho in U.S.A.
LillenasKids.com

Cast

Tommy: He is the oldest boy who has been raised in church and is a bit sarcastic and rough around the edges.

Lucy: She is articulate and wants the best of everything. She and Suzy are best friends.

Suzie: She is competitive and is Lucy's best friend.

Sam: He is a typical competitive, rowdy boy and a little younger than Tommy.

Lillie: A little bit younger than the others. She is very soft spoken and sweet.

Miss Becky: She is energetic and has a contemporary look. Children relate to her very well and she is loved and respected by her students.

Contents

A Christmas Carol *with* Carol Medley 4
Includes: A Christmas Carol – Hark! the Herald Angels Sing –
Joy to the World – O Come, All Ye Faithful

Drama 19

The Bells of Hope 21

Drama 26

God Gave a Gift 27

Drama 33

The Best Gift Is Me 34

Drama 42

Angels Are Rejoicing 44

Drama 50

Give a Gift This Christmas 51

Drama 56

We Wish You a Merry Christmas 57

Production Notes 63

4

(Tonight is the Annual Christmas Caroling/Gift Exchange party. Everyone in Miss Becky's Sunday School class is bringing a gift to exchange with each other. As the cast arrives they put their gifts under the tree. Choir and cast will be dressed in typical Christmas clothing. The cast enters toward the end of the song, from the opposite side of where the set is. They are taking their coats and mufflers off and laughing with one another.)

A Christmas Carol
with
Carol Medley

Words and Music by
PAM ANDREWS
Arranged by John DeVries

Copyright © 2003 by Pilot Point Music (ASCAP). All rights reserved.
Administered by The Copyright Company, PO Box 128139, Nashville, TN 37212-8139.

PLEASE NOTE: Copying of this product is NOT covered by CCLI licenses. For CCLI information call 1-800-234-2446.

*Words by CHARLES WESLEY; Music by FELIX MENDELSSOHN. Arr. © 2003 by Pilot Point Music (ASCAP). All rights reserved. Administered by The Copyright Company, PO Box 128139, Nashville, TN 37212-8139.

*Words, Latin Hymn; attr. to JOHN F. WADE; Music attr. to JOHN F. WADE. Arr. © 2003 by Pilot Point Music (ASCAP). All rights reserved. Administered by The Copyright Company, PO Box 128139, Nashville, TN 37212-8139.

MISS BECKY: Wow! You guys sound great! Did you all have fun caroling tonight?

EVERYBODY: Yeah! It was fun!

LUCY: Except for when Tommy hid behind Mr. Wilson's nativity. He was making loud moo-ing sounds the entire time we were singing "Away in a Manger"!

(EVERYBODY *giggles and snickers.*)

TOMMY: Ah Lucy, I was just trying to create a moooooood!

(*More giggles and laughs*)

SUZIE: Well, how about Sam running from house to house just so he could be first in line to get whatever goodies were being handed out?!

SAM: Suzie, you're just jealous 'cause I beat you every time!

SUZIE: Did not!

SAM: Did too!

SUZIE: Did not!

SAM: Did too!

MISS BECKY: OK, you two, that's enough. Why don't you go help with the hot cocoa while we get ready to decorate the Christmas tree?

SUZIE & SAM: Do we have too?

MISS BECKY: Uh-huh! Tommy, will you grab that box of decorations over there, while Lucy helps me with the garland?

LILLIE: What can I do Miss Becky?

MISS BECKY: You get to choose the music for the tree decorating.

LILLIE: Hmm . . . I think I know exactly the one I want!

TOMMY: No offense Miss Becky, but I think this tree is kinda . . . hopeless!

LUCY: Tommy!

TOMMY: What?

LUCY: That's not very nice.

MISS BECKY: Well, it may not look like much now, but just wait until we're finished!
Lillie, you ready with that music?

LILLIE: I sure am!

MISS BECKY: C'mon everybody, let's decorate!!

(Music begins. LUCY and MISS BECKY string the garland around first and then the rest join in by hanging the bulbs on the tree. The lights are already on the tree. SUZIE and SAM bring in mugs and set them down on the table. At the end of the song they plug in the lights. EVERYONE steps back and admires their work by cheering and clapping!)

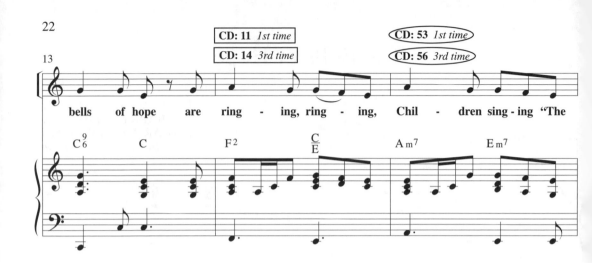
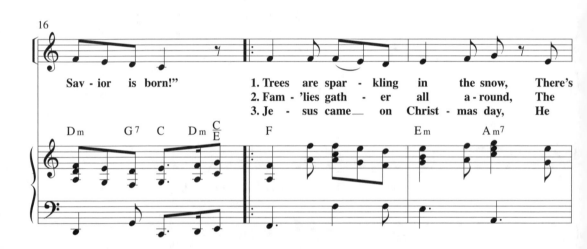

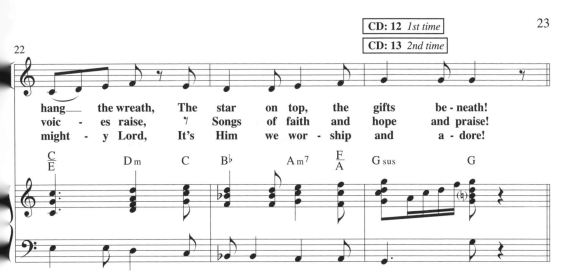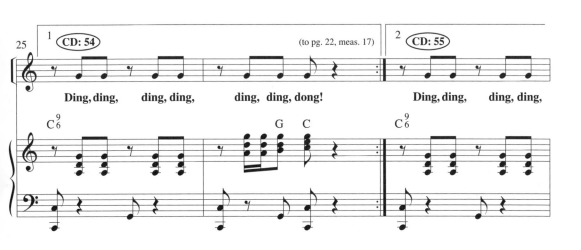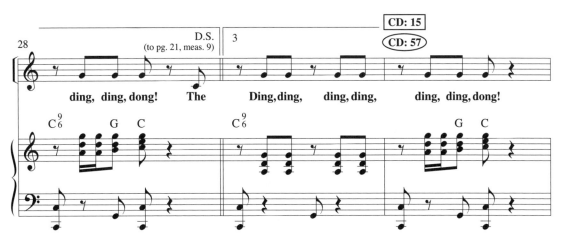

26

MISS BECKY: So what do you think now, Tommy?

TOMMY: It's pretty awesome! Guess it wasn't so hopeless after all.

MISS BECKY: It's amazing how a little bit of help can completely change things. Which brings me to a very important part of this evening's annual Caroling and Gift Exchange Party.

CHILDREN *(chanting)*: Presents! Presents! Presents! *(They all laugh.)*

SUZIE *(half whispering)*: Hey Lucy, just so you know, our presents are right behind the tree. I hid 'em so that no one would take 'em.

LUCY: Great idea! Who ever gets there first needs to grab both of them so we don't get stuck with some lame gift like we did last year. Deal?

(SUZIE and LUCY shake hands.)

SUZIE: Deal! Don't you just love Christmas?!!

TOMMY: Hey Sam. See that big ol' present right there in front of the tree?

SAM *(draws it out)*: Yeah . . .

TOMMY: Well, I've got dibs on it. It's mine bro, all mine.

SAM: Not if I get there first it isn't!

MISS BECKY: OK, listen up everybody. Before we open our presents, I'd like to talk to you about something.

TOMMY: Uh-oh. This can't be good.

MISS BECKY: Does anyone remember what Pastor Mike talked about in church last week?

LILLIE: I remember! He called it "The Great Gift Exchange!"

MISS BECKY: That's right! God gave the gift of His son Jesus, to us. He even gave Him a special name, Immanuel, which means, God with us. He wants us to know that He will never, ever leave us.

(Music begins. During the song the cast can sing along. You can also have some of your cast members sing some solos or use choir members to sing the solos.)

God Gave a Gift

**Words and Music by
C. BARNY ROBERTSON
and CARTER ROBERTSON**
Arr. by C. Barny Robertson

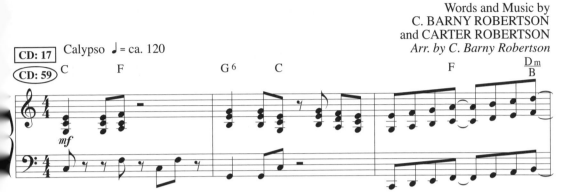

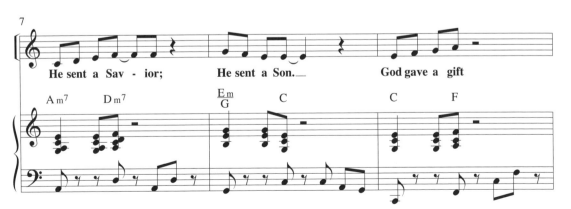

Copyright © 1999 by PsalmSinger Music (BMI). All rights reserved.
Administered by The Copyright Company, PO Box 128139, Nashville, TN 37212-8139.

PLEASE NOTE: Copying of this product is NOT covered by CCLI licenses. For CCLI information call 1-800-234-2446.

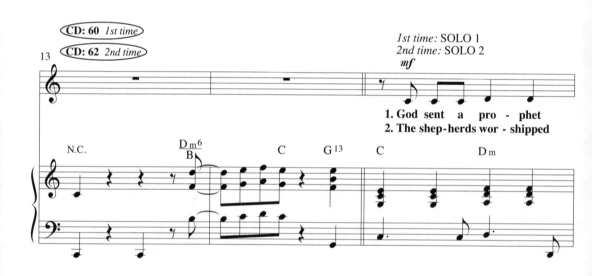

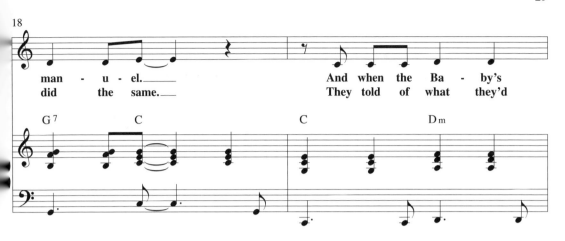
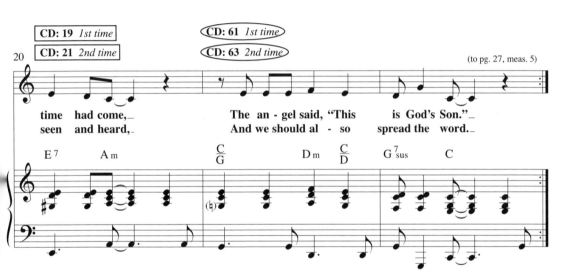
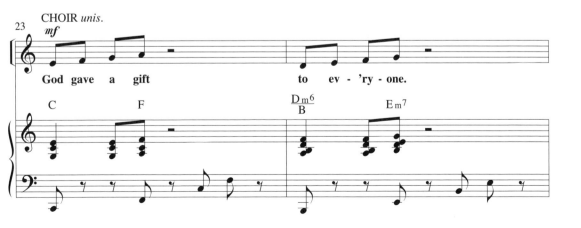

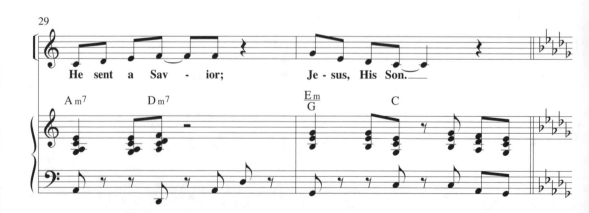

38

to ev - 'ry - one. He sent a Sav - ior;

ev - 'ry - one. He sent a Sav - ior;

$\frac{E\flat m6}{C}$ Fm7 B♭m7 E♭m7

40

Je - sus, His Son.___ He sent a Sav - ior;

Je - sus, His Son.___ He sent a Sav - ior;

$\frac{Fm}{A\flat}$ D♭ B♭m7 E♭m7

42

Je - sus, His Son.

Je - sus, His Son.

$\frac{D\flat}{A\flat}$ A♭13 N.C. D♭ G♭ $\frac{A\flat}{C}$ D♭ N.C.

8va - - - - - - - - - -

SAM: So, I've got a question.

MISS BECKY: Go for it!

SAM: What did we give God?

MISS BECKY: That's the amazing part. God gives us Jesus and in exchange we give Jesus *(pause)* our sin.

EVERYBODY: What?!

SUZIE: I don't get it.

LUCY: Sounds like He got the lame gift.

MISS BECKY: Well, that might be how we see it, but thankfully, that's not how He sees it. The writer of Hebrews tells us to keep our eyes on Jesus, who for, get this, who for the joy set before Him, endured the cross.

SAM: OK, now I really don't get it!

MISS BECKY: You see Sam, Jesus could have stayed in Heaven. But He knew He was the only one who could save us from our sins. He loves us so much and wants us to be with Him, that He exchanged His throne for a manger, and eventually the cross. He paid the price for all of the things we've done wrong.

LILLIE: Miss Becky, I love Jesus. I wish I could give Him the best gift ever.

MISS BECKY: You can, Lillie. We all can. We all have the choice to accept forgiveness from Jesus and give Him our hearts.

(As the song begins, the cast sings sit in a semi-circle facing the audience. You can use whatever furniture you've decided on for the living room, chairs, loveseat etc. The children will sing along with the choir.)

The Best Gift Is Me

Words and Music by
PAM ANDREWS
Arr. by John M. DeVries

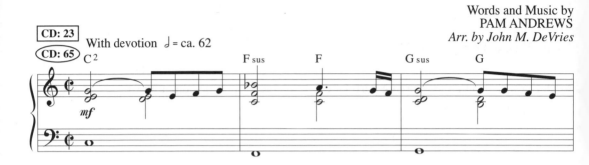

Copyright © 2004 by Pilot Point Music (ASCAP). All rights reserved.
Administered by The Copyright Company, PO Box 128139, Nashville, TN 37212-8139.

PLEASE NOTE: Copying of this product is NOT covered by CCLI licenses. For CCLI information call 1-800-234-2446.

LUCY: Miss Becky, what you said, well *(pause)* it sorta got me thinking.

MISS BECKY: I'm listening.

LUCY: Well, it seems like all I've been thinking about lately is myself. I mean, you should see my Christmas list this year!

SUZIE: I've seen it. Trust me. It's a book!

(Everyone laughs.)

LUCY: The funny thing is . . . I can't even remember half the stuff I got last year. I do remember Christmas Eve service though. I prayed and asked Jesus into my life. It was the best Christmas ever!

MISS BECKY: It's so easy to get distracted this time of year. We all do it. But it's not too late to choose to make this Christmas different.

TOMMY: I've gotta say somethin'.

SUZIE: You're not gonna moo, are you?

(Everyone laughs.)

TOMMY: No. I was just thinkin', even though I've been goin' to church since I was a baby, I've never really asked Jesus to forgive my sin and be my Savior.

MISS BECKY: Would you like to?

TOMMY: Yeah, I really would.

MISS BECKY: Oh Tommy, that's great. Kids, let's kneel down with Tommy as he prays. Just remember, all you have to do is talk to Him from your heart in your own words. I'm right here if you need any help.

(EVERYONE kneels. SAM puts his hand on TOMMY'S shoulder.)

TOMMY: Dear God, it's me Tommy. I've kinda been pretending to know You but I don't want to pretend any more. Will You please forgive me of my sin and be my Savior? I'm glad You're with me. Thank You. Amen!

EVERYBODY: AMEN!

TOMMY: Hey Sam, sorry for acting like such a jerk earlier. If you want the big gift, it's all yours bro. You know what? This makes me feel kinda good.

MISS BECKY: Well, when you have Jesus, the greatest gift of all, you don't need anything else. Kids, did you know that the Bible says when one sinner repents that all heaven rejoices?!

LUCY: Well they must really be having a party tonight!

(EVERYBODY laughs and cheers with a few high-fives as the song begins.)

Angels Are Rejoicing
(They're Having a Party)

Words and Music by
C. BARNY ROBERTSON
and CARTER ROBERTSON
Arr. by C. Barny Robertson

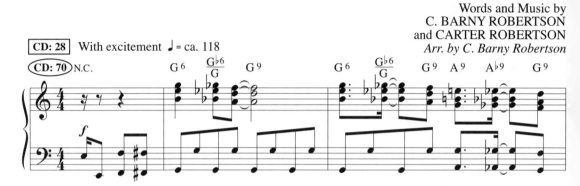

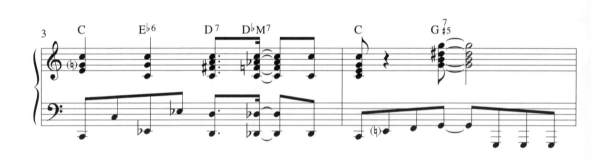

Copyright © 1999 by PsalmSinger Music (BMI). All rights reserved.
Administered by The Copyright Company, PO Box 128139, Nashville, TN 37212-8139.

PLEASE NOTE: Copying of this product is NOT covered by CCLI licenses. For CCLI information call 1-800-234-2446.

45

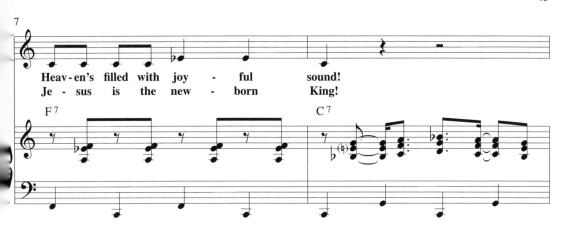
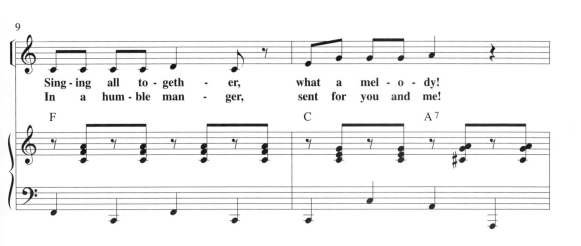
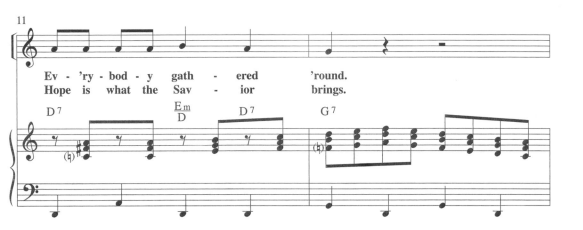

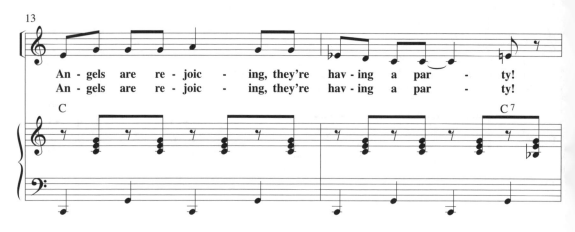

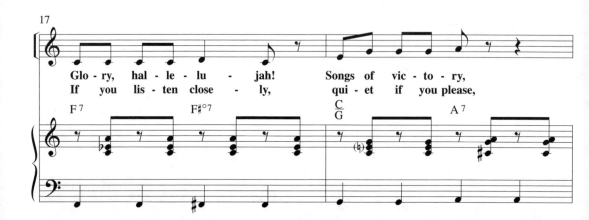

50

MISS BECKY: Looks like it's time for everyone to choose a gift from under the tree!

SAM: Finally!

EVERYBODY: Yeah! Presents!

SUZIE: Hey wait, everybody! Lucy has a really good idea.

MISS BECKY: OK, let's hear it.

LUCY: Well, we don't really need any more presents do we? I don't know about your house but there's no room left under our tree.

SUZIE: C'mon Lucy, tell 'em your idea.

LUCY: I was thinking it might be fun to take all these presents to the family shelter downtown. My Mom volunteers there and she's there right now!

LILLIE: Hey, why don't we go caroling at the shelter and then afterwards hand out the presents?!

MISS BECKY: What do you think, team?

EVERYBODY: That's great! Yeah! Let's do it!

MISS BECKY: I am so proud of all of you! Giving your gifts to people who have nothing but their gratitude to give you in return, is a beautiful picture of what Jesus did for us.

(Music begins. Each member of the cast picks up a gift from under the tree as they sing along.)

Give a Gift This Christmas

Words and Music by
PAM ANDREWS
Arr. by John DeVries

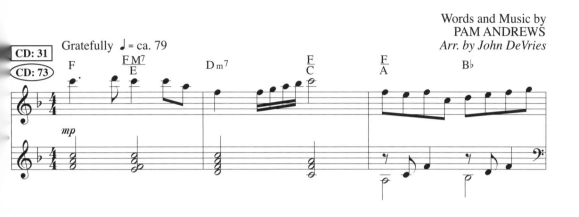

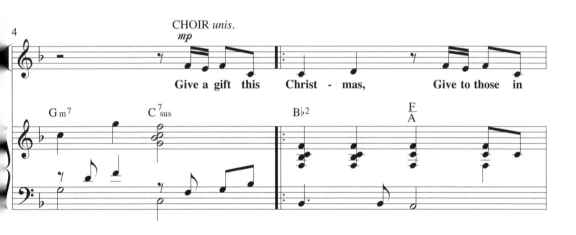

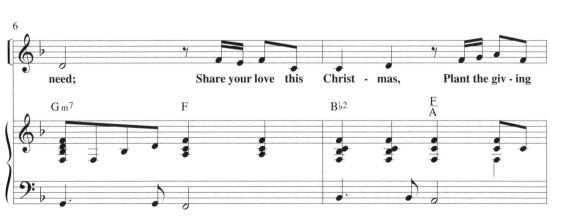

Copyright © 2006 by Pilot Point Music (ASCAP). All rights reserved.
Administered by The Copyright Company, PO Box 128139, Nashville, TN 37212-8139.

PLEASE NOTE: Copying of this product is NOT covered by CCLI licenses. For CCLI information call 1-800-234-2446.

22

us;

Gave His life so now we all can

$\frac{Gm}{B\flat}$ A sus A Dm $\frac{A}{C\sharp}$ $\frac{Dm}{C}$ $\frac{Dm}{B}$

CD: 36
CD: 78

24

cresc.

trust and know Him.

$\frac{Gm}{B\flat}$ Gm^7 C Am^7

cresc.

26

mf

Give a gift this Christ - mas, Give to those in

$\frac{C}{D}$ C^2 $\frac{G}{B}$

mf

28

need; Share your love this Christ - mas, Plant the giv - ing

Am^7 G C^2 $\frac{G}{B}$

TOMMY: It really is the "great gift exchange", isn't it Miss Becky?!

MISS BECKY: It sure is Tommy, it sure is! Well, let's pack up all these gifts, get our coats on and go!!

SUZIE: Dibs on the front seat!

SAM: Not if I get to the van first!

LILLIE: Merry Christmas, everybody!

EVERYBODY: Merry Christmas!!

(Music begins. The cast sings with choir as they put their coats on and put gifts in a box. During the song they could go out in the audience and pass out candy and then return to the stage.)

We Wish You a Merry Christmas

Traditional

Traditional English Melody
Arr. by John DeVries

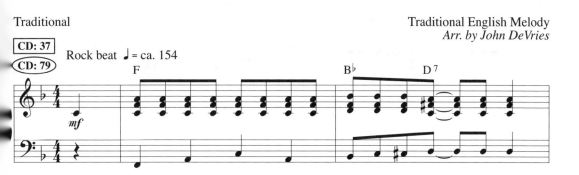

Arr. © 2003 by Pilot Point Music (ASCAP). All rights reserved.
Administered by The Copyright Company, PO Box 128139, Nashville, TN 37212-8139.

PLEASE NOTE: Copying of this product is NOT covered by CCLI licenses. For CCLI information call 1-800-234-2446.

PRODUCTION NOTES

CAST

The cast is a group of kids from Miss Becky's Sunday School class.

TOMMY: He is the oldest boy who has been raised in church and is a bit sarcastic and rough around the edges.

LUCY: She is articulate and wants the best of everything. She and Suzy are best friends.

SUZIE: She is competitive and is Lucy's best friend.

SAM: He is a typical competitive, rowdy boy and a little younger than Tommy.

LILLIE: A little bit younger than the others. She is very soft spoken and sweet.

MISS BECKY: She is energetic and has a contemporary look. Children relate to her very well and she is loved and respected by her students.

SETTING

A simple living room that is decorated for Christmas set up either downstage left or right, with the choir upstage center. There is a tree set to the side that has no decorations on it except for the lights. You can use a pre-lit tree. There is a box of decorations near by. Tonight is the Annual Christmas Caroling / Gift Exchange party at Miss Becky's house.

COSTUMES

Dress Choir and Cast in typical casual Christmas clothing. (Mufflers, gloves, hats etc.)

PROPS

Chairs	Christmas mugs
Loveseat	Christmas tree (preferably pre-lit)
Coffee table	Christmas decorations

SUGGESTIONS

Consider engaging your community or congregation by having them bring canned goods to the concert which will help to stock your church pantry or community charity. The Cast members and ushers could collect them during the last song or you could have a display set up in your lobby of the charity where the goods will be donated.

T-SHIRTS

To purchase The Great Gift Exchange T-shirts, please contact:

Personalized Gift & Apparel
Tom Roland, Owner
(888) 898-6172
Website: www.pg4u.com
Email: info@pg4u.com

OR you can download the T-shirt art from the Lillenas website to create your own shirts.

MOVEMENTS

There are movements available for The Great Gift Exchange online at lillenaskids.com. Just look up the musical by title and scroll down to "Performance Details" and you'll find a free downloadable PDF file.

Please visit our website to download all movements, T-shirt art, and free clip-art.
www.lillenaskids.com